The History and Activities of the
COLONIES

Margaret C. Hall

Heinemann Library
Chicago, Illinois

© 2006 Heinemann Library,
a division of Reed Elsevier, Inc.
Chicago, Illinois

Customer Service 888-454-2279
Visit our website at www.heinemannraintree.com

Designed by Richard Parker and Tinstar Design Ltd (www.tinstar.co.uk)
Printed and bound in China by WKT Company Limited

10 09 08 07 06
10 9 8 7 6 5 4 3 2 1

Library of Congress Cataloging-in-Publication Data

Hall, Margaret, 1947-
   The history and activities of the Colonies / Margaret C. Hall.
      p. cm. -- (Hands-on American history)
   Includes bibliographical references and index.
   ISBN 1-4034-6053-1 -- ISBN 1-4034-6060-4 (pbk.)
   1. United States--History--Colonial period, ca. 1600-1775--Study and teaching--Activity programs--Juvenile literature. 2. United States--Social life and customs--To 1775--Study and teaching--Activity programs--Juvenile literature. I. Title. II. Series.
   E188.H23 2006
   973.2--dc22
                              2004003878

Acknowledgments
The author and publishers are grateful to the following for permission to reproduce copyright material:
Alamy Images pp. 24 (JG Photography), 26 (ShadowWorks); Bridgeman Art Library pp. 6 (Private Collection, © Bonhams, London, UK), 20 (Pollock Toy Museum, London); Corbis pp. 10, 17 (Bettmann), 11; Getty Images pp. 8 (Hulton Archive), 7 (Michael Springer), 18 (MPI); Glasgow University Library p. 5; Harcourt Education pp. 19, 23, 25 (Janet Moran); North Wind Picture Archives pp. 9, 15, 16; Peter Newark's American Photos pp. 13, 14; Photographers Direct p. 12 (Michael P. Gadomski).

Cover photographs by North Wind Picture Archive and Corbis/Bettmann

Contents

Some words are shown in bold, **like this**. You can find out what they mean by looking in the Glossary.

Chapter 1: What Were the Colonies?

During the 1600s, many Europeans sailed to North America. They called it the New World. They came from England, Holland, Germany, France, Spain, and other countries.

The travelers had different reasons for making the difficult journey. Some came to find gold or to claim land. Others were searching for religious freedom.

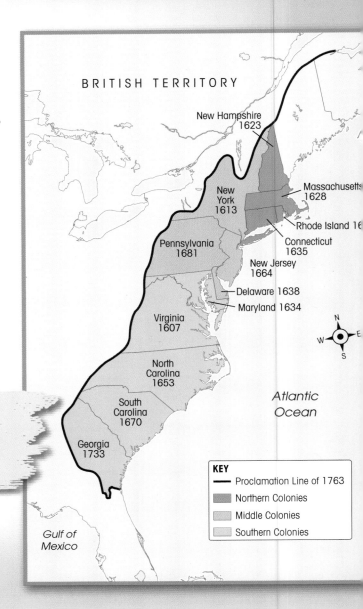

This map shows the thirteen original American colonies.

BRITISH TERRITORY

New Hampshire 1623

New York 1613

Massachusetts 1628

Rhode Island 16

Pennsylvania 1681

Connecticut 1635

New Jersey 1664

Delaware 1638

Maryland 1634

Virginia 1607

North Carolina 1653

Atlantic Ocean

South Carolina 1670

Georgia 1733

KEY
— Proclamation Line of 1763
Northern Colonies
Middle Colonies
Southern Colonies

Gulf of Mexico

TIME LINE

1607
English colonists arrive at Jamestown.

1619
Virginia colonists elect representatives to make laws.

1620
Puritans **found** Plymouth Colony.

1626
Dutch colonists found New Amsterdam.

1634
Cecil Calvert, Lord Baltimore, founds Maryland.

The first permanent **colony** in the New World was at Jamestown, Virginia. A group of English businessmen provided money to start the settlement. They hoped to make money if the colonists found gold to send back to England. The Jamestown colonists did not find gold, but they did start new lives in a new land.

THE MYSTERY OF ROANOKE ISLAND

In 1587 an English colony was established on Roanoke Island, near North Carolina. Roanoke's governor returned to England for supplies. Because a war broke out between England and Spain, he could not return until 1590. When he returned, the colony was deserted and the colonists were gone. The mystery of what happened has never been solved.

Between 1607 and 1670, English settlers established twelve colonies on what would become known as the East Coast. These colonies, along with Georgia in 1732, were the thirteen original colonies. They later became the United States of America.

1634	1664	1681	1732	1776
Roger Williams founds Providence, Rhode Island.	England takes control of New Amsterdam and renames it New York.	William Penn founds Pennsylvania.	James Oglethorpe founds Georgia.	The colonies declare themselves independent of England.

Religion and the colonies

In 1620 a religious group known as **Puritans** came to North America. They **founded**, or established, Plymouth **Colony** in what is now Massachusetts. The Puritans did not approve of the policies of the leaders of England. They came to the New World to live in a place where they could have religious freedom.

The early colonists were not prepared for living in the wilderness. Many people died from starvation or disease. Those who survived sent back stories about their lives and about the land. Despite the hardships, other people were eager to come to America. They saw it as a land of opportunity.

Many colonists came to America to be able to practice their religion freely. So religion was an important part of daily life. However, the religion differed from place to place. In New England, most of the early colonists were Puritans. In the Southern and Middle colonies, most people were Catholic, Jewish, **Quaker**, or part of a Protestant group.

A 19th century artist's idea of what the Puritan arrival looked like.

For most people, Sunday was spent at church. Some sermons lasted so long that listeners fell asleep!

Although many colonists came to the New World for religious freedom, having different religions caused some problems in the colonies. For example, many Puritans didn't believe people should practice any other religion. Roger Williams, a Puritan minister and writer, thought that it was wrong to harass other people because of their beliefs. His religious tolerance made Puritan leaders in Massachusetts very angry, and he was forced to leave the colony. In 1636 Williams bought land from Native Americans and founded the colony of Rhode Island.

Plymouth Rock is a popular tourist spot in Massachussetts.

PLYMOUTH ROCK

The Mayflower arrived in Massachussetts in 1620. Many people talk about Plymouth Rock as the ship's landing place. The first references to this rock did not appear until almost 100 years after the ship landed. It is unclear if the ship actually landed on the rock or if it landed somewhere else nearby.

At first, **colonial** communities were small and far apart. As more people settled in the colonies, communities grew larger and spread out. Some colonists moved on to start new towns. There were also people who traveled west, toward the Appalachian Mountains.

As communities became larger, people no longer needed to provide everything for themselves. People made and sold

COLONIAL CITIES

In 1700 Boston was the only large city in the colonies. However, by 1760, other cities were larger. In fact, Philadelphia became one of the largest cities under British control.

City	Colony	Population
Philadelphia	Pennsylvania	about 23,000
New York	New York	about 18,000
Boston	Massachusetts	about 16,000
Charleston	South Carolina	about 8,000

Early settlers carry lumber and raise the walls of the stockade fort at Jamestown, Virginia, the first permanent English settlement in America.

PENNSYLVANIA

The English king repaid a debt to William Penn by giving Penn land in America. Penn belonged to a religious group called Quakers. He started a colony where Quakers had religious freedom. He called it Pennsylvania, which means "Penn's Woods."

things such as shoes, hats, barrels, or furniture. Ships from the colonies traveled to Europe and Asia with cargoes of tobacco, fish, and lumber. They returned with goods that could not be found in the colonies, such as sugar and tea. Colonists then bought these items from storekeepers.

Most of the thirteen colonies were royal colonies. Governors chosen by the English king ruled them. In Rhode Island and Connecticut, people chose representatives who then picked governors. Maryland, Pennsylvania, and Delaware were proprietorships. These colonies were each owned by an individual who chose the colony's leaders.

In England, men who owned land elected representatives who made laws for the country. The colonists were also English **citizens**. They expected to have this same right. No matter how a colony's leaders were chosen, the people felt they should have a voice in who made the laws.

Chapter 2: Daily Life in the Colonies

The **colonists** spent most of their time trying to survive in their new environment. They needed to provide their own food, clothing, and shelter.

The colonists hunted animals such as deer, beaver, and rabbits. They used the meat for food and the skins or fur for clothing. Most colonial families also owned cows for their milk and chickens for meat and eggs. They grew vegetables like corn and squash and gathered wild nuts and berries.

The colonists planned for the long, cold winters. They preserved meat by drying or salting it. They dried fruits and berries to use later. They stored vegetables like squash and pumpkins in cool root cellars where they wouldn't rot.

In this Colonial kitchen, servants and the mistress are both working.

This house on Nantucket Island is the only remaining building from the original 17th-century English settlement.

Only a few colonists could afford to get clothing sent to them from Europe. In most cases, women made thread and cloth from wool and plant fibers such as cotton and flax. They used this cloth to make clothing for their families. Men wore tight-fitting pants called breeches and long-sleeved shirts. Women wore long dresses. When they were small, both boys and girls wore long dresses called petticoats. Starting around the age of six, children dressed more like adults.

The early colonists had nothing except what they brought with them from Europe. They had to build homes from materials found nearby. The first homes they built were simple. Some were lean-tos made from branches or shelters similar to Native American wigwams.

As soon as possible, colonists built better homes using the many trees in the area. The homes usually had a single room with a dirt floor. Fireplaces were used for cooking and heating. Some homes had lofts for sleeping and storage. As the colonies grew, people built homes more like the ones they had left behind in Europe.

In the **colonies**, family members depended on one another for survival. Everyone worked in and outside the home to provide for the family, even the children. Many of the chores were divided between men and women.

Many families had land to be farmed. Men and boys plowed the land, then planted, tended to, and harvested the crops. Men also spent time building furniture, repairing equipment, and looking after the livestock. Women and girls did chores centered around the home. They cooked the food, sewed clothes, and raised animals such as chickens and ducks. They also made soap, candles, and other things needed for the home.

School days

In the early colonies, all children were expected to learn to read. Boys had lessons in Latin, grammar, penmanship (handwriting), and math. Their teachers were always men.

These modern girls are demonstrating colonial candle-making.

IMPORTANCE OF EDUCATION

Education was especially important to the **Puritans.** Harvard College was **founded** in Massachusetts Bay Colony in 1636. This was only sixteen years after the first colonist arrived in Plymouth. The colony passed laws about education. One law said that parents must teach their children to read. Another said that any town with more than 50 families had to start a school and hire a teacher.

An early school in Delaware. The boy in the corner is being punished for not knowing his lessons.

Most boys went to school for just a few years. Then they left to learn a trade such as making furniture or blacksmithing. However, some boys went on to college. They studied law and became lawyers. Or they studied religion and became ministers.

Girls learned to read at home or at dame schools. A dame school was a school for young children, usually six to eight years old. Women ran these schools in their homes. Very young boys sometimes went to dame schools as well. Wealthy boys were often educated at home by their parents or private tutors. Some wealthy girls had tutors as well and learned to read and write in Greek and Latin.

Chapter 3: Relaxation in the Colonies

In all the North American **colonies**, life was centered around work. There was very little time to relax. It was part of the **Puritans**' religious beliefs to frown upon time spent away from work. So, the colonists found ways to have fun while working. The colonists called these activities frolics.

When townspeople came together to build a house, it was a time to be social. During corn harvests, both men and women gathered for husking bees. The men took the husk off the corn and talked about the weather, crops, and other news. The women shared recipes and information while cooking a big meal, which was shared when the job was done. Children were often given the corncobs for making dolls.

This painting shows Puritan families going to church together.

A painting of Puritan leader John Davenport celebrating his first Sunday in New Haven, Connecticut.

Going into town was another way to see other people and get the news of the day. The colonists would gather together for town meetings and court days. During court days, the townspeople could find out who was getting married, or who was being accused of a crime. The colonists also used this time to visit shopkeepers to pay their debts.

The only day when no work was done was Sunday, which was set aside as a day of rest. The Puritans followed strict rules that no one could work from 3:00 P.M. on Saturday until sunset on Sunday. Families would attend church, or meeting houses, for most of the day, stopping for a meal at noon. During the services, all the boys sat together away from their families. Girls sat near their mothers.

Children

Although **colonial** children worked hard, they found time for fun. In the summer, they enjoyed games like hopscotch, leapfrog, and hide-and-seek. They had toys such as marbles and tops. One toy was called a bilbo catcher. It was a stick with a cup at one end and a pointed spike on the other. A ball with a hole in it was tied to the bilbo catcher. Children tried to catch the ball in the cup or on the spike.

When winter arrived in the Northern colonies, the children there spent some of their time ice skating or sledding. In the Southern colonies, there was no snow or ice, so the families spent more time indoors, dancing and playing cards.

This hand-stitched sampler is signed Margaret Crawford, February 15, 1795.

In colonial times, there were no team sports like baseball and basketball. Men and boys would instead gather to hunt rabbits and foxes on horseback.

Sewing was also a way to pass the time in colonial days. Religion was an important part of learning to sew. Girls practiced different sewing stitches by making pictures with thread. These pictures were called samplers. A sampler's design often included sayings from the Bible, letters of the alphabet, and the name and age of the girl.

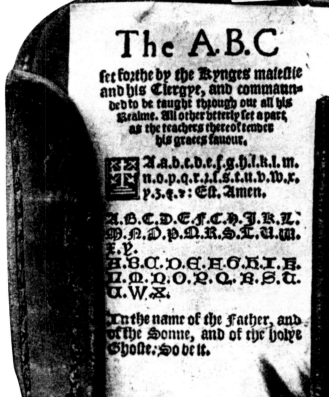

An original hornbook for teaching the alphabet.

HORNBOOKS

Colonial children did not have many books to read. Paper was too expensive. Most children used hornbooks. A hornbook was a sheet of heavy paper printed with letters and numbers. A thin layer of horn from a deer or other horned animal protected the paper. The horn was so thin that the print could be read through it.

17

Chapter 4: Hands-on History

B y doing the activities in this chapter, you will get a feel for what life was like for people in **colonial** times.

Recipe: Make Hasty Pudding

When the colonists arrived in the New World, they were not alone. Native Americans had lived in the land for many years. Some of the Native Americans taught the colonists how to survive by using the land. They introduced the colonists to an important new crop: corn.

Hasty pudding was a popular English dish made with wheat flour or oatmeal. These ingredients were hard to get in the colonies, so cooks began using cornmeal instead. You can try making this old colonial recipe yourself.

Native Americans and Colonists trade at Jamestown.

INGREDIENTS AND SUPPLIES

- double boiler saucepan
- 1 teaspoon salt
- 1 cup (230 grams) yellow cornmeal
- milk
- maple syrup, molasses, or honey

1. Fill the bottom half of the double boiler halfway with water. Place on the stove on high heat.

2. While the water is coming to a boil, combine the salt and another 4 cups (950 milliliters) of water in the top half of the double boiler.

3. Heat the salt and water on another burner until it begins to boil.

4. Place the top half of the double boiler on the bottom half, over the boiling water.

5. Sprinkle the cornmeal into the top level of the double boiler, a little at a time. Stir constantly.

6. Cook over the boiling water for about 30 minutes, until thick. Stir occasionally.

7. Spoon warm pudding into bowls and pour milk over it. Add maple syrup, molasses, or honey to sweeten the pudding.

Activity: Make a Corncob Puppet

Children in the **colonies** usually made their own toys. Girls made dolls from sticks, or at harvest time, they would use corncobs. Corncob dolls remained popular well into the 19th century. Corncobs were easy to get. A store bought doll was considered a luxury few people could afford. Try making a corncob puppet of your own.

Corncob dolls were popular throught U.S. history.

1. Use markers to draw a face on the side of one end of the corncob.

2. Cut a circle of cloth. The circle should be about 8 inches (20 centimeters) across.

3. Fold the cloth in half so that you have a half circle. Cut a smaller half circle from the top of the fold (See Picture A). Before you cut, make sure the hole in the center will be large enough to fit over the corncob. Unfold the cloth, and you now have a donut-shaped piece (See Picture B).

WARNING !

Make sure to read all the directions before starting the project.

SUPPLIES

- dry corncob with kernels removed (can be purchased at a craft store)
- permanent markers
- square scrap of cloth at least 9 by 9 inches (22 by 22 centimeters)
- scissors
- corn silk, colored yarn, or construction paper
- glue

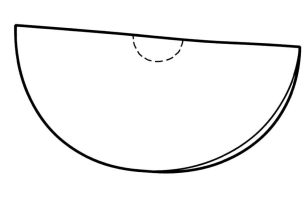

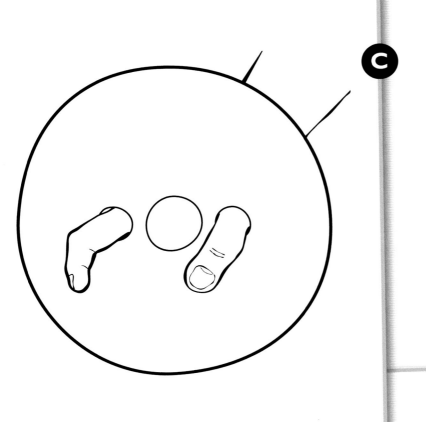

C

4. Refold the piece of cloth. Repeat step three to make two smaller holes on either side of the big hole. These holes should be big enough for your index fingers to fit through (See Picture C).

5. Slide the cloth over the cob.

D

glue

6. Glue corn silk, yarn, or construction paper to the top of the cob to make hair (See Picture D). What else can you do to decorate the puppet?

7. Holding the cob, stick your fingers through the smaller holes to make the puppet's arms.

Activity: Make a Natural Dye

The cloth made by **colonial** women was dull in color. Colonists couldn't afford expensive dyes like the ones used in England. Instead, they made dye from plants that grew nearby. Different plants and flowers produced different colors. Try making some dye yourself. Then use it to dye cloth.

This colonial dress is from the 1730s.

SUPPLIES

- smocks or aprons
- 1 cup fresh cranberries
- 2 cups water
- large stainless steel pot and stove, or electric cooking pot
- wooden spoon
- strainer
- large bowl
- 9-inch (23-centimeter) square unbleached muslin cloth that has been washed and dried
- old newspapers or towels

1. Combine the cranberries and water in a large pot.

2. Cook over medium heat for about 20 minutes. (Ask an adult for help.)

3. Use the spoon to crush the cranberries inside the pot.

4. Cook on low heat for about 15 minutes longer.

5. Strain the mixture into a large bowl. Then throw away the cranberries that remain in the strainer.

6. Place the muslin cloth in the dye. Stir it and let it sit for about 10 minutes.

7. Remove the cloth and hang it to dry. Place the old newspapers or towels under the hanging cloth to catch any drips. *This project makes a red dye. What other plants could you use to make other colors of dye?*

Activity: Make a Quill Pen

When the **colonists** needed to send messages, they wrote letters. Letters were written on heavy paper using quill pens. These pens did not have ink inside them like the pens used today. The colonists used the long feathers from geese and other large birds as quills for writing. The tip of the feather was sharpened—like a pencil—and dipped into an inkwell.

WARNING !

Make sure to read all the directions before starting the project.

1. Let the quill soak in warm, soapy water for about 15 minutes.

2. Ask an adult to help you trim off 2 inches of the bottom feathers of the quill to create a smooth stalk to hold.

3. Cut off the end of the quill stalk at an angle. This will be the point, or nib, of your quill pen. (See picture A)

A

4. Use a straight pin to clean out the inside of the stalk. Work carefully so you don't crack the nib.

5. Now cut a small slit in the nib. This slit will help control the ink flow. (See Picture B)

6. Dip the nib of the quill into the ink. Press the nib gently onto the felt to remove any extra ink.

B

7. Hold your quill pen at a slant and practice writing on paper. Experiment by holding the pen at different angles and using different amounts of pressure.

8. When your quill pen runs dry, dip the nib into the ink again, blot the extra ink onto the felt, and continue writing.

9. If the nib wears down, follow steps 3 through 5 to cut another one. Your pen will be like new again.

10. When you are used to using the quill pen, try practicing the fancy letters and numbers shown here. (See picture C) *Does writing with a quill pen change the kinds of things you write? Would you write the same letter on email as you would with a quill pen? Why or why not?*

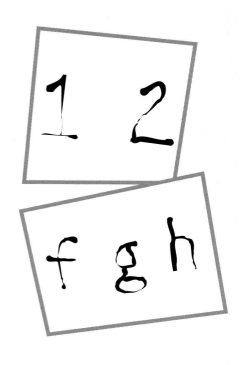

C

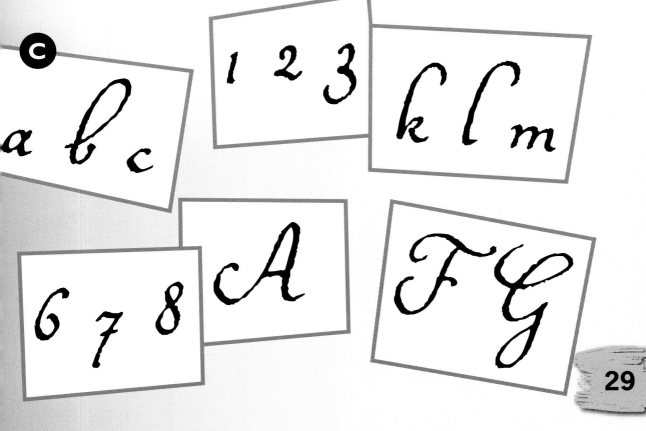

citizen person who lives in an area, and is protected by its government

colony territory that is owned or ruled by another country. Someone who lives in a colony is called a colonist.

found to set up or establish

Puritan member of a Christian group from the 1500s-1600s that opposed the religious customs of the English government

Quaker member of a Christian group that does not believe in priests or ministers. Quakers also do not believe in war or fighting.

More Books to Read

Samuel, Charlie. *Home Life in Colonial America*. New York: Rosen Publishing, 2003.

Stefoff, Rebecca. *American Voices from Colonial Life*. New York: Benchmark Books, 2003.

A Note to Teachers

The instructions for these projects are designed to allow students to work as independently as possible. However, it is always a good idea to make a prototype before assigning any project, so that students can see how their own work will look when completed. Prior to introducing these projects, teachers should collect and prepare the materials and be ready for any modifications that may be necessary. Participating in the project-making process will help teachers understand the directions and be ready to assist students with difficult steps. Teachers might also choose to adapt or modify the lessons to better suit the needs of an individual student or class. No one knows what levels of achievement students will reach better than their teacher.

While it is preferable for students to work as independently as possible, there is some flexibility in regards to project materials and tools. They can vary according to what is available. For instance, while standard white glue may be most familiar to students, there might be times when a teacher will choose to speed up a project by using a hot glue gun to fasten materials for students. Likewise, while a project may call for leather cord, it is feasible in most instances to substitute vinyl cord or even yarn or rope. Acrylic paint may be recommended because it adheres better to a material like felt or plastic, but other types of paint would be useable as well. Circles can be drawn with a compass, or simply by tracing a cup, roll of tape, or other circular object. Obviously, allowing students a broad spectrum of creativity and opportunities to problem-solve within the parameters of a given project will encourage their critical thinking skills most fully.

Each project contains an italicized question somewhere in the directions. These questions are meant to be thought-provoking and promote discussion while students work on the project.

Index